Origins

Pet Play

Claire Llewellyn ■ Jonatronix

OXFORD
UNIVERSITY PRESS

Do you have a pet?

cat

dog

Pets like to play.
Playing keeps them fit and happy.

mouse

budgie

My cat Moggy loves to play!

Here are some toys for pets.

ball

toy mouse

wheel

swing

house

Who plays with a
mouse like this?

5

A cat!

This cat loves her toy mouse!

It likes to catch the mouse.

Who plays with a ball like this?

A dog!

If you throw the ball, the dog runs after it. Then it brings the ball back.

Go boy!

Who plays on a swing like this?

It sits on the swing
and holds on with its feet.

Who plays in a
house like this?

A hamster!

Ant's hamster would love this!

It runs in and out of the window and door.

12

Who likes to play on a wheel?

A mouse!

The mouse runs on the wheel. It turns the wheel with its feet.

All pets like to play. It keeps them fit and happy.

I like to play, too.
Playing with my friends is the
best fun of all!